A NATIVE AMERICAN FEAST

A Native American Feast

BY Lucille Recht Penner

WITH ILLUSTRATIONS
SELECTED BY THE AUTHOR

Simon & Schuster Books for Young Readers

SIMON & SCHUSTER BOOKS FOR YOUNG READERS
An imprint of Simon & Schuster Children's Publishing Division
1230 Avenue of the Americas
New York, New York 10020

First edition
Designed by Beth Tondreau Design
Printed in the United States of America
10   9   8   7   6   5   4   3   2

The text of this book is set in 14 point Janson.
The illustrations are reproductions of photographs, woodcuts,
engravings, and paintings.

*The title page shows a Northeastern Indian using the jawbone of
a deer to scrape corn off the cob; painting by Ernest Smith.*

LIBRARY OF CONGRESS CATALOGING-IN-PUBLICATION DATA
Penner, Lucille Recht.
A Native American feast / by Lucille Recht Penner; with photos and
illustrations selected by the author. — 1st ed.
p.   cm.
Includes index.
ISBN 0-02-770902-7
1. Indians of North America—Food.   2. Indian cookery.
3. Indians of North America—Social life and customs.
I. Title.
E98.F7P46 1994
394.1'089'97—dc20   94-10336

To all Native American cooks

Acknowledgments

For their help with my research, I am grateful to: Roberta Barg of the Tucson-Pima Library; the American Museum of Natural History; the Arizona Historical Society; the Five Civilized Tribes Museum; the Iroquois Indian Museum; the Museum of the Cherokee Indian; the Museum of Florida History; the National Museum of the American Indian; the New York State Historical Association; the North Carolina Department of Cultural Resources; Robert Abbe Museum of Stone Age Antiquities; the Seminole-Miccosukee Photographic Archive; the State Museum of Pennsylvania; and the Washington State Historical Society. I thank the Baxter Lane Company for permission to include the recipes for Wojapi and Wagmiza Wasna from *Indian Cookin'* by Herb Walker. Recipes for Thumbprint Bread and Hopi Blue Marbles were adapted from *Hopi Cookery* by Juanita Tiger Kavena, copyright

1980, by permission of the University of Arizona Press. The recipe for Pueblo Peach Crisp is adapted by permission of the Museum of New Mexico Press from *Pueblo Indian Cookbook* by Phyllis Hughes, copyright 1972. Special thanks to Gayle Harrison Hartmann, editor of *Kiva*; Carolyn Wolf, head of public services of the Stevens-German Library; and Dr. Richard Haan of Hartwick College.

Making Piki Bread; *photograph by Kate Cory*

Contents

A NATIVE AMERICAN FEAST

Introduction

When the first European settlers arrived in North America almost four hundred years ago, they nearly starved to death.

But the Native Americans—whom the Europeans called Indians—seemed to have plenty to eat. How did they do it? The Indians' skill at getting and preparing food amazed the settlers.

European scientists described the plants the Native Americans ate. Artists drew pictures of them hunting, fishing, farming, and eating. And when settlers wrote to relatives back across the ocean, they often mentioned Native American food.

These descriptions, drawings, and letters still provide fascinating information. Further information has been dug from the earth by archaeologists. Animal bones, clamshells, and plant pollen show what Native Americans ate hundreds and thousands of years ago.

Native American eating habits changed slowly over time—and then changed rapidly when the Europeans arrived. Along with the Europeans came European animals, such as the sheep. Some tribes, like the Navajo, became shepherds, with a diet rich in mutton.

One of the most useful new foods that the Europeans brought to America was wheat. New fruits, too, arrived with the settlers. Apples spread across the continent faster than the settlers them-selves! When pioneers reached the West, they found apple trees already growing beside Native American villages. Other new fruits that Native Americans loved were peaches and watermelons. The Hopi called watermelons "horse melons," because, they said, a fresh one smelled like a sweaty horse.

When tribes were forced to move long distances, people's diets changed again. This had happened in the past when one tribe defeated another in war. But it happened much more after the European settle-ment.

Many tribes were pushed westward. Some Eastern tribes that had lived by farming became buf-falo hunters when they moved to the Great Plains.

The story of Native American food is exciting

Plains buffalo hunt

and constantly changing. Some Native American dishes, like hickory nut soup and fried squash blossoms, may seem strange to many of us today. Yet others, like baked beans, succotash, and roast turkey, are familiar. We are the heirs of Native American cooks who were the first to prepare some of our favorite foods.

CAUTION

Cook with an adult helper. Ask the adult to pour and carry hot foods, and to help you use sharp tools for cutting and slicing.

Hickory Nut Soup

William Bartram was a naturalist who traveled in the Southeast in the eighteenth century. He wrote many descriptions of Native American plants, including those used as food.

Native Americans made him welcome and served him wonderful meals. The Creeks, he reported, loved the nuts of the hickory tree. "I have seen," he wrote, "above an hundred bushels of these nuts belonging to one family."

INGREDIENTS

4   cups water
1½ cups hickory nut butter*
1   tablespoon sweet butter
2   tablespoons honey
    Salt and pepper
¼   cup hickory nuts, chopped

Bring the water to a boil. Stir in the nut butter, sweet butter, and honey. Reduce the heat. Simmer, stirring often, until the soup is smooth and heated through. Add salt and pepper to taste. Pour into 4 bowls and garnish with chopped nuts.

Serves 4

*If you don't have hickory nut butter, you may use peanut butter instead.

Green Succotash

According to an old legend, corn, beans, and squash are sisters. Their mother is the earth and their father is the sun.

Each sister has a spirit that sometimes takes the form of a beautiful girl. The three spirits need to live together in order to be happy.

The oldest, the Spirit of the Corn, wears silken tassels, which rustle when she moves. The Spirit of the Bean, dressed in clinging green leaves, twines around her sister and leans on her. The Spirit of the Squash, the youngest, wears a crown of golden blossoms and wanders at her older sisters' feet.

This charming legend arose because corn, beans, and squash were grown together in the fields. Bean vines were trained to climb the cornstalks. Squash was planted in between.

Most Native American farmers—all the way from the green forests of the Northeast to the dry deserts of the Southwest—raised corn, beans, and squash. They often cooked them in the same pot to make succotash.

INGREDIENTS

  1 *butternut squash*
  4 *ears of green corn**
1½ *cups lima beans***
    Salt and pepper
    Butter

Wash and dry the squash. Cut it in half. Scoop out the seeds and the flesh that clings to them. Cut the squash into small pieces. Peel the pieces and place them in a heavy kettle. Add enough cold water to cover the squash. Bring it to a boil, reduce the heat, cover, and simmer until the squash is tender, about 30 minutes.

Slice the kernels of corn from the cobs. Add the corn to the squash. Stir in the lima beans and continue simmering until the corn and beans are tender, about 15 minutes.

Drain the vegetables. Toss them with salt, pepper, and butter.

Serves 4

*Green corn is corn that has been picked just before it is fully ripe. If green corn is not available, substitute ripe corn.

**If fresh lima beans are not available, substitute a 10-ounce package of frozen ones.

Indian Fishing Trip *by John White*

Pueblo Peach Crisp

INGREDIENTS

6	*ripe peaches*
¼	*cup granulated sugar*
½	*teaspoon salt*
¾	*cup flour*
¾	*cup brown sugar*
½	*cup butter*

Preheat the oven to 375°F.

Wash, peel, and slice the peaches. Spread half of the slices in a 9-inch-square baking pan.

Mix the granulated sugar and salt. Sprinkle half the mixture over the peaches in the pan. Cover with the rest of the peaches. Sprinkle with the rest of the granulated sugar mixture.

Mix the flour and brown sugar in a bowl. Cut in the butter with a fork, pastry blender, or your fingers until the mixture feels like coarse bread crumbs. Sprinkle the mixture evenly over the peaches.

Put the pan in the oven and bake until the top is brown and crumbly, about 45 minutes. Serve warm.

Serves 6–8

Mammoths were hunted by Native Americans for their meat and skins.

CHAPTER ONE

Discovering America

A people without history is like the wind

on the buffalo grass.

—SIOUX SAYING

(TRANSLATED BY HARRY HOIJER)

A stone zooms through the air and an animal bellows in pain. A woolly mammoth has been hit in the eye.

The hunter rushes forward to spear the beast. Other hunters join the attack. Soon the mammoth sinks to the earth and dies.

The hunters quickly cut off chunks of meat. Today, they will eat well.

This was how Native Americans hunted long, long ago—so long ago that they hadn't yet invented the bow and arrow. In fact, they had only recently arrived in America.

We know how Europeans crossed the Atlantic in ships. But how did the Native Americans get here? For many thousands of years, there were people in Africa and Europe, people in Asia and Australia, but no people at all in America.

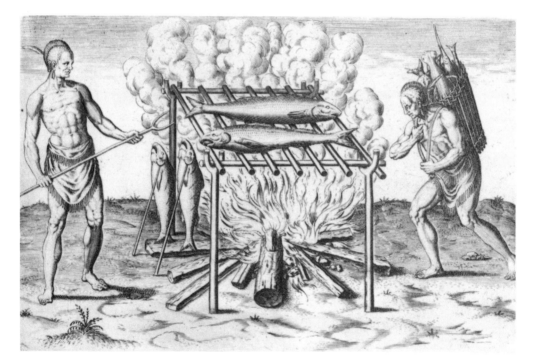

When the first Americans crossed the "land bridge" from Siberia to Alaska, they discovered rivers and lakes teeming with fish.

Then the weather grew very cold. As water froze into icebergs and glaciers, the level of the oceans sank. It sank so low that Alaska and Siberia were joined by a "land bridge" of exposed ocean bottom.

Many Asian animals—including mammoths, bison, and caribou—crossed the land bridge into North America. And hungry human beings followed their prey to the New World.

After thousands of years, the climate grew warmer and much of the ice melted. The oceans rose, and the land bridge was again covered with water. But the animals that had crossed from Asia slowly spread over North and South America. So did the people.

These first Americans discovered forests full of game, rivers and lakes teeming with fish. They crossed mountains crowned with snow and hot, dry deserts, following the animals that provided them with food and skins.

When the herds moved, the hunters and their families trudged after them. They killed so many animals that scientists think this is why certain species, like the mammoth, became extinct.

Thousands of years after these first Americans arrived from Asia, a second wave arrived, this time from Europe. The first permanent English settle-ment was at Jamestown, Virginia, in 1607. Before long, thirteen English colonies lined the Atlantic coast. And in 1776, a new nation, the United States of America, was born.

The Europeans brought guns and steel traps. They killed animals and birds, not only for food but also for their fur and feathers, which they sent back to Europe. They cut down forests to plant crops. Many animals that had made their homes in the forests died.

Passenger pigeons, grizzly bears, and buffalo were all plentiful when the Europeans arrived. There were so many pigeons that when they roosted, trees sometimes snapped under their weight. The pigeons were easy to shoot and trap. They provided great harvests of meat and oil. There seemed an endless supply of them.

But in less than three hundred years, they were gone. The last passenger pigeon died in a zoo in 1914.

Grizzly bears once roamed all over North America. They were hunted for their fat, meat, and fur.

Millions of buffalo grazed the plains before Europeans arrived in America. Native Americans hunted them for their meat and skins, and white men sometimes shot them for sport—even from railroad trains! There were so many buffalo that it could take two days for a herd to pass a particular spot.

But so many buffalo and grizzly bears were hunted that today, few are left.

Many Native Americans died, too. Some died in battle against the newcomers. More died from starvation and disease. Smallpox and measles, which had not existed in America before the Europeans came, sometimes killed entire tribes.

For those who survived, life was different. Many traditional skills were lost. But one tradition that survived was cooking and eating special foods.

As you read this book, you will learn about favorite dishes prepared by tribes in different parts of North America, their ceremonial feasts, their dining manners, and their cooking habits.

And you will learn how to prepare Native American meals for your family, your friends, and yourself.

Grizzly bears were hunted for
their fat, meat, and fur.

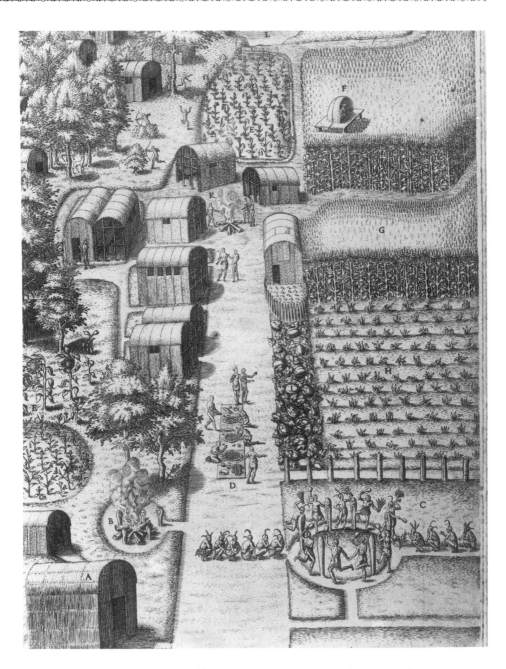

Indian village in North Carolina *by John White*

CHAPTER TWO

A Great Mystery

Lovely! See the cloud appear!
Lovely! See the rain, the rain draw near!
Who spoke?
It was the little corn ear.
High on the top of the stalk.

—ZUNI CORN-GRINDING SONG
(TRANSLATED BY ARNOLD SCHWERNER)

The first Americans were always on the move, looking for things to eat. They hunted animals and gathered wild plants. They knew which greens and roots were best, and which nuts, seeds, and berries. When all the nearby food was eaten, they had to find a new home.

Slowly, people figured out that they didn't have to chase their food. They could make food come to them. They could grow it!

7

*Navajo patterns
and figures*

At first, they scattered seeds and planted roots to provide extra food while they gathered the rest of their supplies.

But as the number of people grew, there still wasn't enough food. They had to grow more and more food themselves. Many people became farmers and settled down to raise crops.

How did they learn to grow plants that are still feeding people all over our planet? We'll never know for sure. It happened too long ago.

Of all the plants they learned to grow, the most mysterious is corn. Wild corn doesn't exist! Several thousands of years ago, ancient farmers *created* corn by crossing the pollen of wild grasses—scientists still aren't sure which ones.

The first corn plants had tiny cobs, no bigger than a dime. But generations of farmers chose seeds from the best plants to produce the next year's crop. Each year, the ears of corn were slightly larger, sweeter, and more tender than the year before. Gradually, farmers created corn as we know it today.

"Indian corn," as the pilgrims called it, wasn't always yellow. There were also red, white, blue, and black varieties. Many people considered blue corn the most delicious of all.

Corn was probably cultivated first in southern Mexico. In time, farmers grew it all over South and North America. Different varieties were developed for hot and cold climates. Nearly everyone ate it— whether they raised their own or not. The Plains

Indians, who didn't grow corn, traded buffalo furs for it.

In most tribes, cooks served corn at nearly every meal. They roasted corn and boiled it. They cooked it with meat, beans, squash, or, in the Southwest, with chili peppers.

They ground it into cornmeal and baked it into cakes. They "milked" it, mashing the juicy kernels into puddings and breads. And some kinds of corn were held over the fire and popped into popcorn.

Among Eastern tribes, corn was so important that an Iroquoian word for corn, *de-o-ha-ko*, means "our life." The Iroquois were a group of tribes in what is now the state of New York. Their villages were surrounded by cornfields. They even *drank* corn that had been boiled to make a thin gruel.

An Iroquois legend tells how people first received corn and beans from Ga-gaah, the crow. Ga-gaah came from the land of the sun, carrying a grain of corn in one ear and a bean in the other. These were planted in the body of Mother Earth and became the life of the people.

But Ga-gaah still flies above the fields and claims his share when the crops ripen. Each time he caws, you can hear him calling his name: "Ga-gaah!"

Roasted Corn on the Cob

INGREDIENTS

4   *ears of corn*
     Melted butter or sunflower oil

Preheat the oven to 350°F.

Gently turn back the husks, but don't tear them off the ears of corn. Pull off the silk or scrub it off with a soft vegetable brush. Smooth the husks back over the corn.

Put the ears in a roasting pan and roast in the oven until the corn is tender, about 45 minutes. Remove.

Wear oven gloves to pull the husks off the corn. *Be careful!* The corn will be very hot.

At mealtime, pass around a bowl of melted butter or sunflower oil to spoon over the corn.

Serves 4

Hopi Kachina,
a doll of the
Calako Mana
(Corn Maiden)

Blue Pinole

Blue pinole, a popular Southwestern cornmeal drink, is flavored with sugar and cinnamon.

INGREDIENTS

1   *cup blue cornmeal*
⅓   *cup sugar*
½   *teaspoon cinnamon*
4   *cups milk*

Preheat the oven to 425°F.

Spread the cornmeal on a heavy cookie sheet. Put it in the oven and bake, *stirring often*, until it turns brown, about 10 to 15 minutes. Remove from the oven and let cool.

When the cornmeal is cool, pour it into a small bowl. Stir in the sugar and cinnamon.

Heat the milk until it simmers gently. Pour it into 4 cups. Stir 4 tablespoons of the cornmeal mixture into each cup of milk. Store leftover pinole in an airtight container.

Serves 4

Thumbprint Bread (Kolatquvil)

These little breads are steamed in a metal colander or steamer set in a pot of boiling water. Originally, Hopi cooks wove dried peach twigs into trays to hold the breads above water as they cooked.

INGREDIENTS

2   *cups coarse cornmeal*
1   *teaspoon baking powder*
1   *tablespoon sugar*
1   *cup boiling water*

Mix cornmeal, baking powder, and sugar.

Add boiling water and stir with a wooden spoon. Gather the dough into a ball and knead it a few times.

Shape teaspoonfuls of the dough into balls. Indent the center of each ball with your thumb.

Put one layer of balls in a metal colander or steamer and set in a pan of boiling water. The water should not touch the balls. You may need to cook several batches.

Cover the pot and simmer the bread for about 8 minutes. Remove with a slotted spoon. Serve warm.

Makes about 30 little breads

Hopi Blue Marbles

Hopi cooks used an ash mixture to deepen the blue color of these "marbles." Baking powder is used instead of ashes in this modern version. If you want the marbles to look very blue, you may add blue food coloring. Blue Marbles were often eaten for breakfast.

INGREDIENTS

1	*cup finely ground blue cornmeal*
1	*teaspoon baking powder*
2	*tablespoons sugar*
4	*drops blue food coloring (optional)*
¾	*cup boiling water*

Mix the cornmeal, baking powder, and sugar.

Stir the food coloring into the boiling water. Stir into the cornmeal mixture, a tablespoonful at a time. Add only enough water so that the dough holds together.

Roll small pieces of the dough into balls the size of marbles.

Heat 4 cups of water to a gentle simmer in a heavy, widemouthed saucepan. Drop in the cornmeal balls and simmer gently, uncovered, for 10 minutes.

Ladle the marbles and some cooking liquid into small bowls and serve at once.

Serves 4

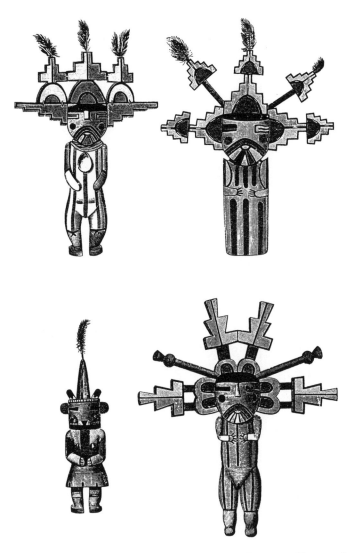

Hopi effigies from Walpi pueblo

Wagmiza Wasna

The Sioux mixed cornmeal and dried berries to make a healthful, sweet snack that you can eat with your hands. Try it instead of candy.

INGREDIENTS

  2   *cups yellow cornmeal*
 1/3 *cup sugar*
  1   *cup dried berries or raisins*
 1/2 *cup corn oil*

Preheat the oven to 375°F.

Spread the cornmeal on a cookie sheet. Toast it in the oven, *stirring often*, until the cornmeal is brown, about 10 to 15 minutes. Let cool. Mix together the browned cornmeal and sugar.

Grind the dried berries or raisins in a food grinder or chop them well.

Heat the oil in a small saucepan over low heat. Stir in the berries or raisins. Cook, stirring, for 2 minutes.

Pour into the cornmeal mixture. Stir gently until the ingredients are well blended. Let cool. Serve at once or store in an airtight container.

Makes 4 cups

CHAPTER THREE

Treasure

Hi hianai hu!
Here on my field
Corn comes forth.
My child takes it and runs,
Happy.
Here on my field
Squash comes forth
My wife takes it and runs,
Singing.

—TOHONO O'ODHAM SONG

Corn wasn't the only treasure that Native Americans gave the world. Among the others were chili peppers, maple sugar, sunflower seeds, and many kinds of beans.

Beans are a wonderful food, easy to grow and rich in protein. They can be dried on the vine and then stored for months or even years. Native American farmers developed kidney, navy, lima, and scarlet runner beans. Fresh or dried beans were eaten in soups and stews, ground into flour, or mashed into cakes.

Pumpkins, too, were among the first foods grown in America. Iroquois cooks baked whole pumpkins in the embers of the fire, then scooped out the flesh and added it to soups and stews. Dried spirals of pumpkin hung from the rafters of every Iroquois house.

The Wichita pounded strips of pumpkin flat, dried them, and wove them into mats. They traded the pumpkin mats to wandering tribes, like the Comanches, who cut off pieces and ate them as they traveled.

Sunflower seeds are another food that Native Americans cultivated. Farmers developed plants with huge flowers and thousands of seeds. Sunflower seeds are very nutritious. Women shelled them, dried them, and ground them into flour.

Peanuts crossed the ocean twice. They were first grown in South America. Spanish explorers found them there and introduced the plant to Africa, where peanuts became an important food.

When African slaves were brought to North America, peanut plants came, too, on slave ships. Soon Indians were growing peanuts in the Southeast. They ate them raw, pounded them into peanut butter, and mixed them with honey to make candy. Sometimes peanuts were roasted, then pounded to make a creamy soup.

Wild rice—a variety of grass—was the principal food of the Ojibwa, who lived near the Great Lakes. For much of the year, the Ojibwa ranged the woods, gathering fruits, nuts, and seeds. Their homes were wigwams, which they moved from place to place in their continual search for food.

But every year when the wild rice ripened, families set up camp on lakeshores and spent weeks harvesting it. Rice grows in shallow water. A paddler

Harvesting Wild Rice *by Seth Eastman*

would propel a canoe slowly along while two harvesters grabbed stalks of rice.

Instead of yanking the plants out by the roots, the harvesters beat them to make the ripe grains fall into the bottom of the canoe. Later, when more grains ripened, they came back and beat the same stalks again.

Ojibwa women boiled wild rice with meat and berries to make thick stews. They ground it into flour for bread. Ducks that came to eat the rice often became duck with rice in Ojibwa cooking pots.

Wild rice could even be popped! And it could be dried, to be saved for the long, cold months of winter. Wild rice was as important to the Ojibwa as corn was to the Iroquois.

For tribes like the Mohave and Pomo in what is now California, acorns were a major crop. If you bit into an acorn straight from an oak tree, it would make you sick. But Native Americans learned how to remove the tannin—the substance that makes acorns so bitter.

In fall, when the acorns ripened, families set up camp near the trees they considered their own. Certain trees belonged to certain families, and they would kill anyone who stole their acorns.

Men and boys climbed the trees and shook the branches. Women and girls gathered the fallen acorns, dried them, removed the shells, and ground them into flour.

Then they leached out the tannin. They scooped a hollow from a little hill of sand and lined it with leaves. Here they placed the acorn flour. They poured water over it again and again until the tannin was washed out. Now the flour was sweet and ready to cook.

Native Americans knew just when wild-growing food was ripe and ready to eat. Women and children gathered mushrooms, greens, and even bark, each in its proper season. They harvested cherries, plums, and a wide variety of wild berries—blueberries, blackberries, strawberries, huckleberries, elderberries, cranberries, and more. Some were eaten fresh and some were dried to be saved for later.

Often, berries were cooked with meat or mixed into batter to make bread. In the Northwest, Kwakiutl cooks whipped soapberries—which foamed like egg whites when they were beaten—to make an unusual dessert.

Besides acorns, Native Americans collected nuts of many other kinds, especially hickory, piñon, and pecan. In the Southeast, Creek women made hickory "milk" by cracking hickory nuts, boiling the meat and shells together, and straining out the solid bits. The remaining liquid, wrote one European visitor, was "as sweet and rich as fresh cream."

Cherokee Bean Balls

The name of the largest Southeastern tribe, the *Cherokee*, means "cave people" in a language used by their neighbors. But the Cherokee call themselves *Ani-yun-wiya*, which means "real people."

After the arrival of the Europeans, many Cherokee built houses, farms, and even plantations. But in the nineteenth century, most of them were driven out of their homes. They were forced to march hundreds of miles to a reservation in Oklahoma. Many died on a route that became known as the Trail of Tears.

INGREDIENTS

$\frac{1}{2}$ *cup dried pinto beans*

$\frac{3}{4}$ *cup cornmeal*

$\frac{1}{2}$ *cup flour*

$\frac{1}{2}$ *teaspoon baking soda*

Wash the beans. Cover them with cold water and soak overnight. Drain. Put them in a heavy saucepan. Add enough boiling water to cover them. Simmer until the beans are tender, about 1 hour. Drain, but save the cooking liquid. Mash the beans.

Mix together the cornmeal, flour, and baking soda.

Mix $\frac{1}{2}$ cup of the cooking liquid into the mashed beans. Stir in the cornmeal mixture and enough of the leftover cooking liquid to make a stiff batter. Roll the batter into walnut-sized balls.

Bring 4 quarts of water to a boil in a heavy kettle. Carefully add the bean balls. Simmer, uncovered, for 30 minutes. Carefully remove the bean balls with a slotted spoon. Pile them on a platter and serve at once.

Makes about 16 balls

Apache Pumpkin with
Sunflower Seeds

The Apache lived by hunting and gathering. They traveled great distances to find food in season. Finally they settled in the Southwest, where they sometimes raided their neighbors, the Hopi and Zuni. Their name comes from the Zuni word for "enemy": *apachu*.

Every year, after the pumpkins sprouted, the Apache sent a young boy to gather juniper berries. When the boy returned, he was blindfolded and brought to the pumpkin field. He threw the juniper berries—a great number of them—in all directions, asking the gods for an equal number of pumpkins.

INGREDIENTS

1   *small pumpkin*
2   *ears of corn*
¼   *cup sunflower seeds, shelled*
1   *tablespoon sunflower oil*

Wash and dry the pumpkin. Cut it in half and scoop out the seeds and the flesh that clings to them. Peel the pumpkin. Cut it into small pieces. Put the pieces in a heavy kettle and add enough cold water to cover them. Bring to a boil. Reduce the heat, cover, and simmer until the pumpkin is almost tender, about 30 minutes.

Cut the kernels of corn from the cobs. Mash them with a fork in a shallow bowl. Add the corn and its juice to the pumpkin. Stir in the sunflower seeds. Continue to simmer until the corn and seeds are tender, about 10 minutes. Drain, toss with sunflower oil, and serve.

Serves 4

Popped Wild Rice

Wild rice is the purplish black seed of a wild grass. Ojibwa women collected the seeds, parched them over a smoky fire, and then poured them into pits lined with animal skins.

Men, wearing special clean moccasins, jumped into the pits and danced on the seeds to loosen the hulls. Then the seeds were tossed in baskets so the wind would blow away the chaff. The Ojibwa called these seeds *meomin*, which means "the good berry."

Unlike popcorn, popped rice is soft and tender.

INGREDIENTS

1   cup wild rice
3   cups water
1   teaspoon oil
½   teaspoon salt

Rinse the rice well in cold water.

Bring 3 cups of water, oil, and salt to a boil in a heavy saucepan. Stir in the rice. Reduce the heat, cover*, and simmer until the rice pops, about 1 hour.

Serves 4

*Don't lift the cover while the rice is cooking or the seeds
will not pop.

Gathering Seeds in the San Joaquin Valley
by Seth Eastman, from a sketch by E. C. Kern, 1865

Zuni Green Chili Stew

The Zuni live in New Mexico. Originally, most of them were farmers. Every day, the men went to their fields to tend crops of chilies, corn, beans, and squash. But the crops actually belonged to the women of the tribe, who owned the seeds of everything the people grew.

INGREDIENTS

- 3 *tablespoons corn oil*
- 2 *pounds lamb, cut in cubes*
- 1 *large onion*
- 3 *mild green chilies or small green peppers*
- 2½ *cups water*
- 3 *ears of corn*
- ½ *cup cornmeal*
- ½ *cup cold water*

Heat the oil in a heavy skillet. Add the lamb cubes and brown them on all sides.

Chop the onion and the green chilies or peppers. Sprinkle them over the meat and add 2½ cups of water. Bring to a boil. Reduce the heat, cover, and simmer for 1 hour.

Cut the kernels off the ears of corn. Add them to the stew and continue simmering for 15 minutes.

Mix the cornmeal and cold water. Add the mixture to the stew and simmer, stirring, until the liquid thickens, about 5 minutes.

Ladle the stew into bowls and serve.

Serves 4–6

Zuni Bean Dance
by Otis Polelonema

Leader of the Mandan Buffalo Bull Society *by Karl Bodmer*

CHAPTER FOUR

The Hunt

Over the whole earth they are coming.
The buffalo are coming, the buffalo are coming.
The Crow has brought the message to the tribe,
The father says so, the father says so.

—SIOUX GHOST DANCE SONG

Huge buffalo thunder over the rolling plains. Behind them pound hunters on beautiful spotted Appaloosa ponies. Arrows fly and an enormous beast drops to the ground. The herd rushes on.

Hunters run to the fallen buffalo and pull out their arrows. The man whose arrow pierces the buffalo's heart is given the best parts—the tongue, the liver, and the fatty hump. Others, whose arrows also struck home, divide up the rest.

Every part of the beast can be used for something, except the heart. When a great hunt is over, hundreds of buffalo hearts are left on the ground. Hunters believe that this will renew the herd.

At first, Plains Indians hunted buffalo on foot. They sneaked up on the herd by covering themselves with the skins of wolves. Buffalo didn't run away from wolves, and were often fooled.

But after they got horses from the Spanish, many Plains people became excellent riders and followed the herds for great distances. Only a few tribes kept permanent homes and grew crops.

Men and boys were the hunters in almost every Native American tribe. They shot, trapped, and speared their prey. They brought home fish, fowl, and many kinds of animals for the cooking pot.

Tribes of the Northeast loved elk and moose meat. In winter, these large, heavy animals moved slowly through the deep snow. Hunters wearing snowshoes could easily catch and kill them. In the Southeast, many people hunted and ate alligators. And some tribes ate dogs—the only domestic animal before the arrival of Europeans.

The Paiute, who lived in the Western desert, caught tiny animals like mice and kangaroo rats with a trap called a deadfall. One rock was balanced on another, with food for bait wedged in between. When a mouse tugged at the bait, the top rock crashed down and killed it.

A bear hunt was much more dramatic. An Iroquois hunter showed his bravery by walking right up to a bear and knocking it on the head with a club. This was extremely dangerous, but considered more honorable than shooting arrows from a safe distance. Bears were prized for their fur, their claws, and their delicious fat. Gallon after gallon of fat could be rendered from a large bear. Today, we eat a lot of fat—butter, cream, ice cream, chocolate—every day. But Native Americans had very little fat in their diet, so they treasured it.

The Inuit hunted musk oxen, reindeer, and caribou—caribou eyes were a special treat, usually saved for the children—but their most important food was seals, which they ate raw. An Inuit hunter would wait for hours beside a seal's breathing hole in the ice. When at last the seal poked up its nose, he quickly stabbed it with his harpoon.

Many tribes hunted insects, too. Even when other game is scarce, insects can always be found. Some tribes cooked ants together with berries and pine-

Iroquois hunter

sap—or mixed them with seeds and ground them into flour. Caterpillars and crickets were eaten raw or roasted.

Other people collected the larvae of flies, dried them, and cooked them in soup. In the Southeast, Cherokee cooks made soup of yellow jacket grubs, fat, and water. Beetles, locusts, wasps in the comb, fleas, and even lice were added to soups and stews.

People who lived near oceans, rivers, lakes, and swamps caught and ate lots of fish. The Kwakiutl, who lived on the shore of the Pacific Ocean, ate fresh or dried salmon almost every day.

But the Hopi of the Southwestern desert never ate fish. It wasn't usually available to them in the dry desert. And if they were offered fish in trade, they still hesitated to eat it. Water was terribly important to them. They needed it to irrigate their crops of corn, beans, and squash. They feared that if they ate fish, the Spirit of the Water would become angry at them.

Sometimes hunters died trying to provide food for their families. The Inuit fished through holes in the ice for trout, salmon, and whitefish. Occasionally an ice floe broke off with a fisherman on it. Then he might float away into the ocean and—when the ice beneath him melted—drown.

Broiled Buffalo Steaks

In the north
the wind
blows
they are walking
the hail
beats
they are walking

—SIOUX SONG OF THE BUFFALO DANCE

Tribes that lived on the Plains sang many beautiful songs about the buffalo, on which they depended for most of their food. Almost every part of the animal went into the cooking pot. Fresh buffalo steak was a special treat.

INGREDIENTS

4   *one-inch-thick sirloin tip buffalo steaks**
     (about 8 ounces each)

Place the steaks on a rack about 6 inches from the broiler. Broil for 3 minutes on one side. Turn and broil the other side for 4 minutes. The steaks will be rare. Cook them longer if you want the meat well-done.

Serves 4

*If you don't have buffalo, you may substitute beefsteaks.

Hokyana Kachina

Venison and Hominy Stew

Comes the deer to my singing,
Comes the deer to my song,
Comes the deer to my singing.

—HUNTING SONG

This simple, delicious stew was a favorite of Southeastern tribes. It was cooked in a clay pot over an open fire.

INGREDIENTS

$\frac{1}{2}$ cup flour
  1 pound venison, cut in 1-inch cubes*
  1 tablespoon corn oil
  2 cups water
  4 peppercorns
  1 bay leaf
  2 cans white hominy (14 $\frac{1}{2}$ ounces each)
    Salt and pepper

Put the flour in a bag. Add the venison cubes and shake to coat them.

Heat the oil in a heavy skillet. Shake the excess

flour off the venison cubes and add them to the skillet. Brown the cubes on all sides.

Add the water, peppercorns, and bay leaf to the skillet. Simmer, covered, until the venison is tender, 1 to 1½ hours.

Drain the hominy. Gently stir it into the meat. Bring the mixture to a boil. Immediately reduce the heat and simmer, uncovered, for 10 minutes. Season with salt and pepper to taste. Ladle the stew into 4 bowls and serve at once.

Serves 4

*If you don't have venison, you may substitute beef.

CHAPTER FIVE

Feast and Famine

Beast of the sea,
Come and offer yourself in the dear early morning!
Beast of the plain,
Come and offer yourself in the dear early morning!

—ESKIMO SONG

For some Native Americans, food was scarce and life was often desperate.

People of the Great Basin—a dry desert lying where Nevada and Utah are today—ate almost anything that flew, crawled, walked, or swam. They hunted mice, rabbits, squirrels, robins, magpies, lizards, snakes, porcupines, and skunks.

They would eat all the food in an area, then move on to search for more. They ate cattail pollen, the pads of the prickly pear cactus, buckberries, and tiny mustard seeds, and used pointed sticks to find edible roots growing underground.

Seeing them hunched over their sticks, settlers gave them the insulting name "Diggers." But the people of the Great Basin were very good at finding hidden food.

Other Native Americans also suffered when food was scarce. When the Iroquois were starving, they made soup from the bark of trees. They stole nuts that squirrels had collected and even took roots from muskrat nests. That was scary, because they believed that muskrats had the power to harm anyone who made them angry.

Among the Sioux and Kiowa of the Great Plains, it was the job of old women to rob the nests of field mice. They took most of the food that the mice had stored, but always left one bean to show their good hearts.

The Tohono O'Odham, living in what is now southern Arizona, didn't have game-filled forests or plains brimming with buffalo. But they were resourceful at finding food in the blistering hot desert. Tohono O'Odham women stewed cactus fruit and flowers in deer fat.

Following rare desert rains, they gathered worms, pinched off an end, and squeezed out the insides. Then they braided the worms, baked them in pits, and finally fried them to make a popular dish.

People of the Great Basin joined in huge grasshopper hunts. First they dug an enormous pit in the ground. Then the hunters spread out in a big circle around it. They beat the ground to frighten the grasshoppers, which leaped into the air. Then the hunters herded them into the pit.

The largest grasshoppers were made into soup or roasted over the fire and eaten like peanuts. But most of the catch was ground into paste and dried to save for the starving days of winter.

In the Arctic, winter was harsh. When snow-storms made it impossible to see, Inuit hunters and fishermen had to stay home. Families lived on the food they had stored.

After that was gone, they began eating their dogs, and then scraps of leather and bone—and finally their animal-skin clothing. Parents sometimes ate nothing at all to save a bit of food for their children.

But for most people, there were good times, too. Then they feasted. Sometimes they ate for days.

Among the Inuit, a favorite feast was the auk, a seabird. Auks weren't cooked—just stuffed in a seal-skin bag and frozen. The bag was passed around and each guest chose an auk that looked especially tasty.

Starting from the bill, he pulled back the skin until it was turned inside out. Then he sucked the tasty oil from the skin, pulled off the feathers, and ate the skin. After that, he ate the flesh and the soft bones. To conclude, he belched loudly to show how greatly he'd enjoyed the meal.

Most feasts were harvest festivals, and corn was the most important harvest. In fact, corn was so important that many tribes had special Green Corn Festivals as soon as the corn began to ripen in the fields. Food and drink were consumed in vast amounts.

But the green corn itself received special treatment. Before the Seminoles ate it, they would purify themselves with a special drink—called the "Black Drink"—that made them vomit. They did this so that the sacred corn would not touch ordinary food inside their bodies.

The Creek Indians considered their Green Corn Festival to be the start of a new year. They built a huge fire in the village and burned all their old clothes, furniture, and leftover food.

Then the people put out their old fires and lit new ones from the great fire. They cooked green corn and offered it to the gods. They themselves feasted on huge platters of roasted corn and venison seasoned with bear fat.

The Salish Indians held a feast to welcome the harvest of wild raspberries. They cooked the first ripe berries in a new pot over a new fire. Everyone stood with eyes closed in a circle around the fire.

The chief made a speech to the Spirit of the

Raspberry Plant, praying for a good harvest. Then the cooked berries were ladled into new wooden bowls and people sat down to eat.

Indians of the Great Plains feasted on the first buffalo of the season. First they prayed to the Spirit of the Buffalo. Then warm buffalo blood, in cups made of buffalo horn, was passed around to be shared by all.

Slices of raw buffalo liver, dipped in the salty juices of the beast's gallbladder, were considered a great treat. Children ate all they could get, and begged for more until it was all gone. Next, the buffalo's skull was cracked and the brains scooped out with a horn spoon. The huge tongue was roasted.

Finally the intestines were removed, turned inside out, and cleaned. They were stuffed with chunks of meat and roasted over the glowing coals of the fire.

In the Northwest, food was plentiful. Each spring, salmon left the sea and swam up rivers and streams to spawn.

People spent weeks catching and cooking them. They baked them in pits lined with seaweed, or roasted them on ironwood spits. Many were preserved by smoking and saved to be eaten later.

But as many as possible were eaten fresh.

Delicious salmon for every meal! And in between meals, roasted salmon tails were available all day, kept warm on a rack above the fire.

Halibut, flounder, herring, sole, sturgeon, seal, otter, and shellfish also came from the sea. Horse clams were so huge that a single one could feed a whole family. Smaller smoked clams were strung into necklaces on fibers of cedar bark. Babies wore them as teething rings.

Fish and animals were preserved by smoking and saved to be eaten later.

The Makah of the Northwest hunted whales from canoes. When they harpooned one, they towed the huge carcass home. The meat and skin were eaten, the blubber was boiled to make oil, and the intestines were saved for water bags.

Because food was plentiful in the Northwest, people had to work only a few months in order to feed themselves for the entire year. They had time to make beautiful carvings, baskets, and blankets, and to become great cooks. And they could afford enormous festivals and parties.

The most impressive of these were the potlatches of the Kwakiutl. Guests at a potlatch stayed for days. They ate and drank—often until they were sick—the best their host could offer.

Meanwhile, the host ordered his slaves to pour dishes of expensive oil on the fire, making it flare so brightly that his guests shrank back from the heat. He did this to prove himself a rich man. For the same reason, he gave his guests many gifts, including oil, furs, and slaves.

Now *they* would have to invite *him* to a potlatch, with similar gifts and destruction of wealth. If they failed to do so, he would have shamed them. They would seem cheap, poor, and ridiculous.

Mouse Cache Soup

INGREDIENTS

4   cups beef broth
¼   cup sunflower seeds, shelled and broken
2   tablespoons sesame seeds
2   tablespoons buckwheat groats
2   tablespoons millet
½   teaspoon salt
¼   teaspoon pepper

Bring the beef broth to a boil in a heavy kettle. Stir in the sunflower seeds, sesame seeds, buckwheat groats, millet, salt, and pepper. Reduce the heat. Cover and simmer for 1 hour. Ladle into 4 bowls and serve at once.

Serves 4

Iroquois Strawberry Drink

When the strawberries are ripe
his creatures thank him.
Thank him in a great feast
and dance ceremony.
Now I ask that the time of strawberries
may return again.

—FROM A SENECA PRAYER OF THANKSGIVING

INGREDIENTS

1   pint ripe strawberries
4   cups water
4   tablespoons maple sugar*

Wash the strawberries and remove the stems and leaves. Cut the berries into small pieces and mash them in a large bowl. Stir in the water and maple sugar. If you like a very smooth drink, puree the mixture in a blender. Chill in the refrigerator or serve at once.

Serves 4

*If you don't have maple sugar, you may use brown sugar.

Mushrooms Cooked in Oil

When mushrooms sprang up, hungry people looked them over carefully. Many mushrooms are poisonous! Women taught their children which ones were safe to eat. Make this recipe with cultivated mushrooms that you buy in the grocery store.

INGREDIENTS

1   pound mushrooms
2   tablespoons corn oil
    Salt and pepper

Scrub the dirt off the mushrooms with a soft vegetable brush. Cut a tiny piece off the end of each stem and throw it away. Slice the clean mushrooms into thin pieces.

Heat the oil in a large skillet. Add the mushroom slices and cook them over medium heat until they are brown. Turn and brown the other side. Season with salt and pepper to taste and serve at once.

Serves 4

CHAPTER SIX

Berries, Flowers, and Bear Fat

Our father, hear us, and our grandfather.
I mention also all those that shine, the
yellow day, the good wind, the good timber,
and the good earth.

All the animals, listen to me under the ground.
Animals above ground, and water animals,
listen to me. We shall eat your remnants of
food. Let them be good.

Let there be long breath and life. Let the people
increase, the children of all ages and the women,
the old men of all ages and the old women. The
food will give us strength whenever the sun runs.

Listen to us, Father, Grandfather. We ask thought,
heart, love, happiness. We are going to eat.

—ARAPAHO PRAYER BEFORE EATING

Native American cooks had the art of mixing delicious foods together to make them more nutritious. Meat and fish were often cooked with fruit, berries, bear fat, vegetables, and even flowers.

Northwestern people added juniper berries to their salmon dishes. The Seminoles of Florida cooked with wild grapes and later with oranges, brought to America from Spain. The Iroquois enriched their stews with huckleberries and blackberries. Among the Pueblos, squash blossoms brightened and flavored the cooking pot.

A thick, red berry bush flourished on the Plains in springtime. Women and children picked huge mounds of the bright berries. They called them buffaloberries, because they were often cooked with buffalo meat.

A favorite combination of foods was pemmican— usually a mixture of dried meat, berries, and melted fat. Packed into rawhide bags, it kept for months and even years. The meat provided protein, the fat was a source of energy, and berries added necessary vitamins. And it tasted so good that children ate it like candy.

Corn—the most important food of all—was often cooked in a solution of water and hardwood ashes.

This added protein and minerals. It also loosened the kernels from their tough hulls. The tender insides, called hominy, were left. Women ground hominy into flour or added it to soups and stews.

What about seasonings? Iroquois cooks used only a little salt. They thought it made people too thirsty. And women believed it made their hair turn gray. Instead, they flavored food with bear fat, bayberries, pepper roots, and wild ginger.

Southeastern Indians liked to dip their meat, fish, or corn bread in a salty-tasting paste of ashes. Choctaws flavored their soups and stews with powdered sassafras leaves. And in the Southwest, Pueblos grew fiery chili peppers, which they included in most recipes—raw, cooked, or ground into powder.

When it came to sweets, the people of the Northeast loved the taste of maple sugar. They boiled maple sap to make a thick, delicious syrup. Then the syrup was poured into molds and left to harden into maple sugar. In parts of the country where maple trees didn't grow, people sometimes drank the sap of other trees, but it wasn't as sweet or as good.

The Pueblos discovered a way to sweeten bread. Young girls with clean mouths were chosen to chew kernels of corn. Their saliva mixed with the corn to form a sugar. They spit the chewed corn into a pot. Then it was pounded into paste, wrapped in corn husks, and baked in the ashes of the fire.

Native Americans took their sweets wherever they could find them. Algonquian-speaking tribes chewed the inner bark of pine trees. Observing this,

Iroquois neighbors called one Algonquian tribe a name that means "they eat logs."

But the favorite sweet of all was honey. Nothing else is so delicious. When a hunter found a beehive, he would kill a deer if he could, remove its insides, and fill the skin with rich, sticky honeycomb to carry home.

Most Native Americans preferred not to drink plain water. Instead, they boiled it with fragrant leaves to make tea. Many tribes boiled cornmeal to make a thin gruel that they drank with their meals. Desert people, who often had to walk a long way for water, sometimes sucked out the sweet juice of cacti.

The Inuit of the frozen North also had a problem getting water. After a snowfall, they could melt snow for a drink. At other times, the only water around was in the form of sea ice. People can't drink salt water. But when the sea freezes in thick sheets, the topmost layer contains little salt. Inuit women chipped it off, brought it home, and melted some whenever the family was thirsty. They said it tasted sweet.

Fried Squash Blossoms

Pick the blossoms just before they open. The large, male blossoms are usually used in this dish.

INGREDIENTS

12   squash blossoms
½   cup milk
1   egg
3   tablespoons flour
½   teaspoon salt
1   tablespoon corn oil

Gently wash the blossoms and pat them dry.

Beat the milk, egg, flour, and salt. Dip each blossom in the mixture. Set on a rack to drain.

Heat the oil in a heavy skillet. Put in the blossoms, a few at a time, and cook until they are golden brown. Turn and cook the other side. Lift them out with a slotted spoon and drain on paper towels.

Serves 4

Pemmican Cakes

The settlers called the meat used in pemmican "beef jerky." According to one story, they gave it this name because it was so tough that you had to *jerk* it out from between your teeth. Making pemmican with beef jerky and bear fat was hard work, but this recipe is easy.

INGREDIENTS

 1   teaspoon butter
 ½   pound ground beef
 1½ tablespoons butter, softened
 ⅓   cup nutmeats, chopped
 ⅓   cup dried cherries or raisins

Heat 1 teaspoon butter in a heavy skillet. Add the ground beef and cook, stirring often, until it is browned. Drain and cool the beef. Put it in a bowl.

Cream the butter. Mix it into the beef. Stir in the nutmeats and cherries or raisins. Divide the mixture into 4 mounds. Spoon each one into a small plastic bag. Squeeze out all the air and fasten the bags. Refrigerate for 2 hours or overnight before eating.

Serves 4

Maple Sugar Drink

*Maple Sugar
is the only thing
that satisfies me.*

—OLD SONG

How was maple sugar discovered?

Long ago, some curious person probably tasted the liquid that ran from a cut in a maple tree. It was sweet and good. So the person used it to boil food. When it was heated, the maple sap thickened into a delicious syrup. And as it cooled, the syrup hardened into sugar.

Soon tribes that lived near maple forests were tapping the trees every year when the sap began to run. Besides using maple sugar to sweeten their food, they mixed it with water to make a delicious drink.

INGREDIENTS

4   *cups water*
½   *cup maple sugar**

Bring the water to a boil. Stir in the sugar, reduce the heat, and simmer for 10 minutes. Remove from the heat, let cool, and serve at once or store in the refrigerator until you are ready to serve.

Serves 4

*If you don't have maple sugar, you may use brown sugar.

Wild Grape Dumplings

These dumplings are cooked in the juice of wild grapes, which gives them a delicious flavor and a beautiful blue color.

When dumplings were served, each person fished one from the cooking pot with a sharp stick and waved it in the air to cool. After the meal, people wiped their dumpling sticks and stuck them into cracks in the wall to save for next time.

INGREDIENTS

- 1 cup flour
- ¼ cup sugar
- 1½ teaspoons baking powder
- ½ teaspoon salt
- 2 tablespoons shortening
- ⅓ cup milk
- 4 cups grape juice

Mix the flour, sugar, baking powder, and salt in a small bowl. Stir in the shortening with a fork, pastry blender, or your fingers until the mixture looks like coarse crumbs.

Stir in the milk. Gather the dough into a ball and

knead it a few times. Heat the grape juice in a heavy, widemouthed saucepan until it simmers gently. While it is heating, roll tablespoonfuls of the dough into balls.

Drop the balls of dough into the simmering juice. Cover and simmer for 15 minutes. Ladle the dumplings and juice into 4 bowls and serve at once.

Serves 4

Inuit Ice Cream

A mixture of berries and whipped seal oil was combined to make an Inuit treat. In this recipe, egg whites are used instead of seal oil, but you may add sardine oil for flavor.

INGREDIENTS

2   *egg whites*
1/2   *cup sugar*
1/8   *cup sardine oil (optional)**
4   *cups blueberries or blackberries*

Beat the egg whites and sugar until the mixture holds soft peaks. If you are using sardine oil, stir it into the egg white mixture. Gently fold in the berries. Spoon into 4 bowls and serve at once.

Serves 4

*You may use the oil from a can of sardines packed in oil. Save the sardines for another dish.

Wojapi

Sioux cooks made this simple fruit pudding with chokecherries that grew wild on the prairie. You may use any fresh cherries or berries.

INGREDIENTS

2   *cups fresh cherries or berries*
1   *cup water*
½   *cup sugar*
½   *cup flour*
4   *whole cherries or berries*

Mash 2 cups of cherries or berries.

Bring the water to a boil. Stir in the sugar and boil 2 minutes.

Add the mashed fruit. Reduce the heat. Stir in the flour and simmer, stirring, until the mixture thickens.

Spoon the pudding into 4 bowls and top each one with a whole cherry or berry. Serve warm or cold.

Serves 4

CHAPTER SEVEN

Lighting the Fire

Pounding, grinding, chopping, smashing—each mouthful a Native American cook served cost a tremendous amount of labor.

Before she even lit the fire, the cook and her family had to hunt or grow or gather, butcher or grind, shell or dry almost everything they ate.

Women and girls prepared the food. Their work seemed never to be done. Corn and acorns had to be pounded with heavy stones to make flour. Grains—

like wild rice—were hulled and winnowed. Seeds and nuts were ground into flour, or smashed and then boiled to extract their oil.

Before an animal could be cooked, it had to be skinned and butchered. This was hard work. A Ute chief named Ouray once became furious at a white official who said the Utes were lazy people. "We work as hard as you do," Chief Ouray said. "Did you ever try skinning a buffalo?"

Fresh meat, sliced into strips, was dried in the sun to preserve it. The drying meat turned black and hard. Before it was cooked, it needed to be softened with more pounding.

To make bread, Hopi women spent hours grinding corn. Three women worked together. The first ground the corn coarsely. The second ground it more finely, and the third ground it yet again, into very fine flour. Often, an old man sang or played the flute to entertain the women as they worked.

After all these jobs were done, it was finally time for the actual cooking. There were three main methods: pit baking, broiling, and boiling.

Pit baking was done underground. A deep hole was lined with stones. Then a fire was built in the hole to make the stones extremely hot. Fresh food—

wrapped in leaves, corn husks, or seaweed to keep it clean—was placed on the hot stones. It was covered up with dirt and left to cook slowly.

Indians of the Southwest baked the roots and hearts of the agave plant in pits. Northwestern tribes pit-baked camas bulbs that women dug up each spring. When the pits were opened, the bulbs had turned into a sweet, sticky brown mass. Everyone feasted heartily. Any leftovers were formed into cakes and dried.

New England tribes pit-baked lobsters, clams, and corn. Even today, a clambake is a favorite New England festivity. By tradition, it is held right on the beach, so the seafood will be at its freshest.

To broil meat, Native Americans pierced it with sharp sticks and held it over the fire. Only green wood was used, so the sticks wouldn't burst into flames. The Kwakiutl built special wooden frames to hold salmon close to the fire.

Pottery vessels, as well as deerskin bags, buffalo stomachs, and birch bark boxes were used by Native Americans for cooking.

A pottery design

When they needed to boil their food, Native Americans used almost anything that held water—clay pots, deerskin bags, wooden bowls, buffalo stomachs, birch bark boxes, and tightly woven baskets.

Most of these would be damaged if they were put right on the flames. Instead, the cook heated stones in a fire. She filled the container with water and added the cooking ingredients.

Then she dropped in the red-hot stones to make the water boil. As the stones cooled, the cook removed them and added freshly heated stones until the food was done.

In addition to baking, broiling, and boiling their food, cooks sometimes fried it on a stone slab set over a fire. They smeared the slab with animal fat, which melted into grease and began to sizzle. Then the cook put on the steaks or corn mush.

This was how Hopi women made piki bread, a delicious pastry. In one motion, the cook dipped her hand into a bowl of cornmeal batter and quickly spread a thin layer on the sizzling stone.

She lifted it off when it was done, spread a new layer, and laid the cooked one on top of it. When she had fried four layers, she rolled them into a cylinder.

A Hopi girl was not considered ready for marriage until she had learned to make piki. The best piki makers, it was said, could have their choice of husbands.

To bake birds and fish and squirrels, the cook sometimes sealed them in their own tiny ovens. Soft clay was smeared all over the little creatures. Then they were laid in the ashes and covered with hot coals. The clay hardened. When the cook broke it with a stone, the feathers, scales, or fur were sticking to it. Inside, ready to eat, was the tender, delicious meat.

Broiled Salmon Steaks with Juniper Berries

Northwestern cooks were said to have more than a hundred different ways of preparing salmon. Most often, it was smoked. People snacked on smoked salmon all day long. The name of one tribe, the *Kwakiutl*, means "Smoke of the World."

INGREDIENTS

Juniper berries
4 *one-inch thick salmon steaks (about 8 ounces each)*
Sunflower oil

Press 5 to 6 juniper berries into each salmon steak. Brush the steaks with sunflower oil. Broil them for 4 minutes. Turn and broil the other side until the fish is done, 6 to 8 minutes.

Serves 4

Boiled Rabbit with Corn Dumplings

In the Great Basin, many families came together for a rabbit hunt. First they strung woven nets at the end of a little canyon. People fanned out around the trap.

At the leader's signal, everyone began to shout. Frightened rabbits sprang up from the grass and were herded toward the nets. Men with clubs rushed up and killed them, sometimes by the hundreds.

Some rabbit meat was boiled. Some was dried and stored in grass-lined pits. The pits were covered with stones, so the meat wouldn't be dug up by coyotes and wolves.

Even the rabbits' bones were used. They were pounded and made into soup.

INGREDIENTS

3 *tablespoons corn oil*
1 *rabbit, cleaned and cut into 8 pieces*
  Salt and black pepper
½ *cup flour*
4 *ears of corn*
1 *cup flour*
¼ *cup cornmeal*

1   *teaspoon baking powder*
½   *teaspoon salt*
¼   *teaspoon red pepper*

Heat the oil in a heavy skillet.

Sprinkle the rabbit pieces with salt and black pepper to taste. Put ½ cup flour in a paper bag. Add the rabbit pieces, a few at a time, and shake to coat them. Put the pieces in the skillet and brown on both sides.

Add just enough water to cover the meat. Bring to a boil. Reduce the heat. Cover and simmer until tender, about 1 hour.

While the meat is cooking, make the dumplings.

Husk the corn and remove the silk. Grate the kernels of corn from the cobs. Put the grated corn and its liquid in a bowl.

Mix the flour, cornmeal, baking powder, salt, and red pepper. Stir it into the grated corn. When the rabbit is cooked, drop tablespoonfuls of the corn mixture onto the simmering stew. Cover and simmer gently until the dumplings are done, about 10 minutes. Use a slotted spoon to place portions of rabbit and dumplings on 4 plates.

Serves 4

Baked Beans with Maple Sugar

Clay pots of beans covered with leaves or seaweed were baked in stone-lined pits.

INGREDIENTS

2   *cups dried kidney beans*
½   *teaspoon salt*
¼   *teaspoon pepper*
¼   *teaspoon dry mustard*
½   *cup maple sugar**

Wash the beans. Put them in a large bowl, cover with cold water, and soak overnight.

Drain the beans. Put them in a heavy kettle and cover with cold water. Bring to a boil. Reduce the heat, cover, and simmer until tender, about 30 minutes. Drain, but save the cooking liquid.

Preheat the oven to 300°F.

Mix the salt, pepper, dry mustard, and maple sugar.

Put the beans in a heavy casserole. Stir in the maple sugar mixture. Pour in 1 cup of the cooking liquid.

Cover the casserole and put it in the oven. Bake for 4 hours, stirring occasionally. If the liquid boils away, add more, 1 cupful at a time.

Remove the cover and bake until all the liquid is absorbed, about 30 minutes.

Serves 4–6

*If you don't have maple sugar, you may use brown sugar.

CHAPTER EIGHT

A Basketful of Water

In the beginning God gave to every people
a cup of clay, and from this cup
they drank their life.

—NORTHERN PAIUTE PROVERB

How can you cook without pots and pans?
Before the Europeans arrived, Native
Americans didn't have iron, steel, or glass.

But they made everything they needed from
wood and bark and plant fibers, from the skins and
horns of animals, from stone and shell and clay.

Clay cooking pots were made in many sizes and
shapes. The Iroquois made pots with pointed bot-
toms. With a twist of the wrist, the cook would stick

a pointed-bottom pot in the ashes of the fire. This dug it firmly into the ground, keeping it upright while the food inside it cooked.

Sometimes food was boiled in baskets. California tribes filled watertight baskets with acorn flour and water. Red-hot stones were added, and the cook stirred the flour until it thickened into mush.

Pomo Indians made baskets—some so big that children could hide in them—decorated with flying geese, rattlesnakes, and other designs. The design never went all the way around the basket. The Pomo believed that anyone who made a basket with a design all the way around it would go blind.

The Iroquois were skilled at making waterproof containers from birch bark. These were rarely used for cooking, because the fire would scorch them. But their light weight made them perfect for carrying food along on trips. Birch bark helps preserve food, and doesn't change its taste.

When Inuit women cooked, they burned fish oil in lamps carved from soapstone to heat the food. Inuit cooking took a long, long time. In winter, the Arctic air was so cold that the food cooled almost as fast as the fire could heat it.

Nature itself provided many containers. Pumpkin

shells and gourds were often used for baking food. And the bladders of animals made good water bags. Inuit used walrus bladders. Plains Indians used buffalo bladders.

Plains women also cooked food in the stomach of a freshly killed buffalo. They filled it with meat, berries, and water and hung it over the fire. After serving as a pot for several meals, the stomach began to fall apart. When that happened, the cook simply served it, along with its contents, at the next meal.

Sometimes the emptied body of a whole animal was used as a storage or cooking container. The Plains Indians cooked huge feasts in buffalo carcasses. Inuit removed the insides of seals and filled them with oil.

When the Kwakiutl had a great harvest of berries, they sometimes cooked them in a canoe! They half filled the canoe with water and poured in the berries. To bring the water to a boil, they added stones that had been heated in a fire.

In the same way, Northwestern tribes used a canoe and red-hot stones to extract the delicious oil of a fish called the eulachon. When the eulachons began to boil, their oil rose to the surface. These fish are so oily that Indians sometimes used them as torches! In fact, another name for the eulachon is "candlefish." It was eulachon oil that Kwakiutl chiefs burned during potlatches to show off their great wealth.

Many tribes made dishes from wood. The Iroquois carved bowls with scenes of war or animal hunts. The Nunivaks of Alaska made beautiful wooden dishes and painted them red with a mixture containing seals' blood. Tlingits from the Northwest steamed thin pieces of cedar and cherry wood to make graceful bentwood boxes and bowls.

It was always polite to eat with your fingers. If you had to pick up something hot, a sharp stick served as a fork. Knives were fashioned from stone. Coastal tribes made spoons out of mussel shells or clamshells, and the Iroquois carved big wooden spoons.

But to scrape corn off the cób, the Iroquois used a special tool—the jawbone of a deer. They even had a joke about it: "The deer chews the corn first."

Each tribe did the best it could with whatever materials were available. Some traded with other tribes for shells or baskets or boxes. They found or made whatever they needed to cook interesting and delicious foods.

Pumpkin Shell Soup

Pumpkins are an excellent food, rich in vitamin A. Native Americans enjoyed them year-round. They dried the meat of fresh pumpkins to preserve it for the cold winter months. They also stored whole pumpkins in pits that they dug below the frost line and lined with birch bark.

This soup is served in a pumpkin shell.

INGREDIENTS

- 1 medium pumpkin
- 4 cups chicken broth
- 4 tablespoons maple sugar*
- ½ teaspoon cinnamon
- ½ teaspoon nutmeg
- ½ teaspoon salt
- 1 large pumpkin

Preheat the oven to 350°F.

Wash and dry the medium pumpkin. Cut it in half. Remove the seeds and the pulp that clings to them.

Place the pumpkin halves, skin side up, on a buttered cookie sheet and bake until tender, about 1 hour.

The pumpkin is cooked when you can easily cut its flesh with a fork.

Let cool. Scrape the pumpkin meat from the skin. Press it through a sieve with the back of a spoon to remove the fibers.

Put the pumpkin meat in a heavy saucepan. Stir in the chicken broth, maple sugar, cinnamon, nutmeg, and salt. Cook the mixture, stirring often, over medium heat until hot.

While the soup is cooking, prepare a pumpkin shell by cutting a circle off the top of the large pumpkin. Remove the top and scoop out the seeds and the pulp that clings to them.

Ladle the soup into the shell. Bring to the table. Serve the soup from the shell.

Serves 3–4

*If you don't have maple sugar, you may use brown sugar.

CHAPTER NINE

Good Manners

"Don't overeat," Seneca parents warned their children, "or bogeyman Longnose will get you."

Children were trained to take small bites with half-closed mouths, to chew and swallow quietly, and not to talk while eating.

Except at feasts, or to show courtesy to their hosts, most Native Americans ate lightly. Greedy eating was bad manners.

One reason people ate little was that food was so hard to prepare. Everything had to be made by hand. Among tribes in southern California, the women began grinding acorn meal as soon as they awoke. Around noon, an acorn gruel would finally be ready. Then the whole hungry family sat down to eat.

The Iroquois ate only one formal meal each day. The cook ladled out the food onto bark dishes. First she served the men, then the women, and last the children. They used their hands to scoop up bits of hominy, meat, and corn bread dipped in grease. Then they praised the cook, whether they liked the food or not. After the meal, all thanked the Creator by striking the ground and holding a fist up toward the sky.

The Cherokee ate two meals a day. Their morning meal was corn mush. At night, they had more mush, broiled fish or meat, or a meat-and-vegetable stew. Between meals, anyone who felt hungry could grab a handful of parched corn. Parched corn is filling and nutritious. Hunters, who had to travel light, sometimes ate nothing else for days.

Like other tribes, the Cherokee took special care in feeding their babies. Babies can't swallow anything too big or hard. So Cherokee mothers made baby food by chewing up nuts and berries. Then they fed the soft, wet mixture to their tiny ones.

Arapaho mothers felt special concern when their babies were ready to learn to talk. Then the babies were fed a meal including eggs from the meadowlark. This food, the Arapaho believed, would help their babies gain the gift of speech. According to an Arapaho legend, meadowlarks spoke Arapaho.

Inuit often ate meat or fish stews. The father reached into the pot and pulled out a hunk of fish or blubber. He cut off a piece and passed it to his wife. She cut off a slice for each of their children.

But guests were always served first! An Inuit would offer a guest even his last bit of food. No matter how good the meal might be, the host would apologize, saying that it wasn't worthy of his guest. The guest, in turn, would praise the food, eat all he could to show how greatly he enjoyed it, and then belch loudly to demonstrate his pleasure.

Many tribes had taboos having to do with food. Some wouldn't eat rattlesnakes, though others greatly enjoyed them. The Blackfeet never ate turtles or frogs, which they believed were creatures of evil.

Fish and fowl were taboo to the Comanches— who especially despised turkeys. Turkeys were cowardly, they believed. Anyone who ate turkey would surely become a coward himself.

Dog meat, too, was taboo to some tribes. But others enjoyed dog. The Cheyenne loved nothing better than a fat puppy, nicely boiled.

Also taboo were twins, which were thought to bring bad luck. People avoided eating twin seeds, twin nuts, or even the two rows of meat lying next to a buffalo's backbone.

Most Native Americans were generous and hospitable. A Creek hunter always gave some of his catch to his parents, and some to the widows and orphans of the town. Seminoles kept extra food in public storehouses. Everyone who needed food—including runaway slaves—could help themselves.

This was good manners, but it was also something more. It was in keeping with the Native American belief that the Creator had provided his bounty—sun and rain, animals and plants—for the good of all. No one should keep the blessing of food for himself alone.

CHAPTER TEN

Thanksgiving

Come to me
come to me
little brother
feed me
feed my family
feed my children

—SALISH SONG

Native Americans believed in good manners not only toward other people, but also toward the food itself, and toward the Creator who had provided it. Comanches thanked the Great Spirit by holding up a morsel of food toward the sky before they ate. Then they burned it as an offering.

When the corn ripened, Cherokee medicine men went to the cornfields and pretended to weep loudly. They were apologizing to the Spirit of the Corn for cutting down the stalks.

In the same way, a hunter apologized to his prey. He explained that he and his family needed the food, and asked the animal's forgiveness for killing it.

Sometimes people honored the spirits of creatures they ate by burning their bones. In the desert Southwest, a hunter who killed a rabbit tried to inhale its last breath. He did this to make himself strong and to keep the spirit of the animal alive.

Among the Kwakiutl, the first bear killed each year was treated with great ceremony. The hunter brought it home and arranged it in a sitting position in the place of honor. He put a ring of cedar bark around it and sprinkled eagle down on its head. Then he invited his friends to a feast. A helping of food was placed in front of the dead bear and speeches of welcome were made to it.

After the meal, the guest of honor was skinned, cut up, and cooked.

When an Inuit hunter brought home a seal, his wife laid it on a bed of fresh snow and poured a drink of water into its mouth. The Spirit of the Seal, the Inuit hoped, would tell others that it had been treated with respect. Then other seals would not be afraid of hunters.

For the first salmon caught each spring, Salish Indians held a special ceremony of thanksgiving.

First they sprinkled the fish with eagle down. They laid it on the riverbank with its head pointing upstream, to show other salmon the way to swim.

Next, children sang the Salmon Song as they carried the fish home from the river. When they arrived in the village, the chief gave a speech of welcome to the salmon. If the first salmon was well treated, the Salish believed, its soul would urge others to follow.

Finally the fish was roasted and given to the children to eat. This was the only time that Salish children were allowed to eat before the grown-ups.

Tribes whose lives depended on the salmon showed respect to the fish's soul by returning its bones to water. One legend told of a rude little boy who simply flung salmon bones into the bushes when he was done eating. Later he went swimming—and drowned.

The Salmon People found him and took him to their underwater village. There they explained that they offered their flesh for humans to use as food. If humans showed gratitude by returning the salmons' bones to water, they could come back to life.

This legend shows the belief of Native Americans that Nature was kind. If treated with respect, it would renew itself and last forever. It would provide life and joy for generation after generation.

We return thanks to our mother, the earth, which sustains us.

We return thanks to the rivers and streams, which supply us with water.

We return thanks to all herbs, which furnish medicines for the cure of our diseases.

We return thanks to the corn, and to her sisters, the bean and squash, which give us life.

We return thanks to the bushes and trees, which provide us with fruit.

We return thanks to the wind, which, moving the air, has banished diseases.

We return thanks to the moon and stars, which have given us their light when the sun was gone.

We return thanks to our grandfather He'-no, that he has protected his grandchildren from witches and reptiles, and has given to us his rain.

We return thanks to the sun, that he has looked on the earth with a beneficent eye.

Lastly, we return thanks to the Great Spirit, in whom is embodied all goodness, and who directs all things for the good of his children.

—IROQUOIS ADDRESS OF THANKSGIVING TO
THE GREAT SPIRIT

Selected Bibliography

Alexandra. The Eskimo Cookbook. *Seattle: Hancock House Publishers, 1977.*

Batsdorf, Carol. The Feast Is Rich. *Bellingham, WA: Whatcom Museum of History and Art, 1980.*

Bierhorst, John. The Sacred Path. *New York: William Morrow and Company, 1983.*

Cox, Beverly, and Martin Jacobs. Spirit of the Harvest: North American Indian Cooking. *New York: Stewart, Tabori and Chang, 1991.*

Cronyn, George. American Indian Poetry. *New York: Fawcett Columbine, 1962.*

Densmore, Frances. How Indians Use Wild Plants for Food, Medicine, and Crafts. *New York: Dover Publications, 1974.*

Driver, Harold E. Indians of North America. *Chicago: University of Chicago Press, 1969.*

Fussell, Betty. The Story of Corn. *New York: Alfred A. Knopf, 1992.*

Hays, Wilma, and R. Vernon. Foods the Indians Gave Us. *New York: Ives Washburn, 1973.*

Hesse, Zora Getmansky. Southwestern Indian Recipe Book. *Palmer Lake, CO: Filter Press, 1973.*

Hughes, Phyllis. Pueblo Indian Cookbook. *Santa Fe: Museum of New Mexico Press, 1972.*

Johnson, Marlene, ed. Iroquois Cookbook. *Allegany Reservation: Peter Doctor Memorial Indian Scholarship Foundation, 1989.*

Kavasch, Barrie. Native Harvests. *New York: Random House, 1977.*

Kavena, Juanita. Hopi Cookery. *Tucson: University of Arizona Press, 1980.*

Kimball, Yeffee, and Jean Anderson. The Art of American Indian Cooking. *New York: Simon and Schuster, 1965.*

Niethammer, Carolyn. American Indian Food and Lore. *New York: Collier Books, 1974.*

Parker, Arthur. The Indian How Book. *New York: George H. Doran Company, 1927.*

————. Parker on the Iroquois. *New York: Syracuse University Press, 1968.*

Reader's Digest. America's Fascinating Indian Heritage. *Pleasantville, NY: Reader's Digest Association, 1978.*

Sharpe, Ed, and Thomas B. Underwood. American Indian Cooking and Herb Lore. *Cherokee, NC: Cherokee Publication, 1973.*

Tunis, Edwin. Indians. *New York: Thomas Y. Crowell, 1959.*

Ulmer, Mary, and Samuel E. Beck, eds. Cherokee Cooklore. *Cherokee, NC: Mary and Goingback Chiltoskey, 1951.*

Utter, Jack. American Indians: Answers to Today's Questions. *Lake Ann, MI: National Woodlands Publishing Company, 1993.*

Van Doren, Mark, ed. Travels of William Bartram. *New York: Dover Publications, 1928.*

Verrill, A. Hyatt. Foods America Gave the World. *Boston: L. C. Page and Company, 1937.*

Walker, Herb. Indian Cookin'. *Amarillo, TX: Baxter Lane Company, 1977.*

Whistler, Frances Lambert. Indian Cookin. *Chattanooga, TN: Nowega Press, 1973.*

Williamson, Darcy, and Lisa Railsback. Cooking with Spirit: North American Indian Food and Fact. *Bend, OR: Maverick Publications, 1988.*

Witthoft, John. Green Corn Ceremonialism in the Eastern Woodlands. *Ann Arbor: University of Michigan Press, 1949.*

Index